Written with Love

Written with Love

Passionate love-letters selected by

Barbara Cartland

HUTCHINSON

London Melbourne Sydney Auckland Johannesburg

Hutchinson & Co. (Publishers) Ltd
An imprint of the Hutchinson Publishing Group
17-21 Conway Street, London W1P 5HL

Hutchinson Group (Australia) Pty Ltd
30-32 Cremorne Street, Richmond South, Victoria 3121
PO Box 151, Broadway, New South Wales 2007

Hutchinson Group (NZ) Ltd
32-34 View Road, PO Box 40-086, Glenfield, Auckland 10

Hutchinson Group (SA) Pty Ltd
PO Box 337, Bergvlei 2012, South Africa

Designed and produced for Hutchinson & Co by
Bellew & Higton Publishers Ltd,
17-21 Conway Street, London W1P 5HL

First published 1981

Typeset by V & M Graphics Ltd, Aylesbury, Bucks
Printed in Great Britain

ISBN 0 09 146620 2

About the Editor

Barbara Cartland, the world's most famous romantic novelist, who is also an historian, playwright, lecturer, political speaker and television personality, has now written over 300 books and sold 200 million over the world.

She has also had many historical works published and has written four autobiographies as well as the biography of her mother and that of her brother, Ronald Cartland, who was the first Member of Parliament to be killed in the last war. This book has a preface by Sir Winston Churchill and has just been republished with an introduction by Sir Arthur Bryant.

She has recently completed a novel *Love at the Helm*, with the help and inspiration of the late Admiral of the Fleet, the Earl Mountbatten of Burma. This is being sold for the Mountbatten Memorial Trust.

Miss Cartland in 1978 sang *An Album of Love Songs* with the Royal Philharmonic Orchestra.

In 1976, by writing twenty-one books, she broke the world record and has continued for the following four years with twenty-four, twenty, twenty-three and twenty-four. In the *Guinness Book of Records* she is listed as the world's top-selling author.

In private life Barbara Cartland, who is a Dame of the Order of St John of Jerusalem, Chairman of the St John Council in Hertfordshire and Deputy President of the St John Ambulance Brigade, has fought for better conditions and salaries for Midwives and Nurses.

She has championed the cause for old people, had the law altered regarding gypsies and founded the first Romany Gypsy camp in the world.

Barbara Cartland is deeply interested in Vitamin Therapy and is President of the National Association for Health.

She has a magazine, *Barbara Cartland's World of Romance*, now being published in the USA and 'Barbara Cartland's Romantic World Tours' operate from America in conjunction with British Airways.

Acknowledgements

The editor and publishers would like to thank the following: Her Majesty the Queen for Her Gracious Permission to republish extracts from letters of King George V and extracts from Queen Victoria's Journal; John Murray (Publishers) Ltd for permission to quote from *Byron: A Self Portrait* edited by Peter Quennell; the Trustees of the Estate of Mrs Patrick Campbell for permission to quote extracts from *Bernard Shaw & Mrs Patrick Campbell: Their Correspondence* published by Victor Gollancz; George Weidenfeld and Nicolson Ltd and Doubleday & Co Inc for permission to quote from *Lady Sackville* by Susan Mary Alsop; Anthony Glyn for permission to quote from *Elinor Glyn*; the Society of Authors on behalf of the Estates of Katherine Mansfield and John Middleton Murray; the Executors of the Estate of James Joyce, Jonathan Cape and Viking Penguin Inc for permission to quote from *A Portrait of the Artist as a Young Man*; A. J. P. Taylor for permission to quote from *My Darling Pussy, The Letters of Lloyd George & Frances Stevenson* 1913-1941 edited by A. J. P. Taylor.

The Eva Peron letters are taken from *El 45* by Felix Luna published by Editorial Sudamericana and *El Ultimo Peron* by Esteban Peicovich published by Editorial Planeta.

The Clementine Churchill Winston letters are reproduced from *Clementine Churchill* by Mary Soames published by Cassell Limited and with the kind permission of Times Newspapers Limited. The same extracts copyright 1979 Times Newspapers Limited are reprinted by permission of Houghton Mifflin Company.

Every effort has been made to trace holders of copyright material reproduced in this book. If, however, the editor and publishers have inadvertently omitted to contact any such copyright owners, they will be happy to pay the standard reproduction fee on application.

Contents

Foreword by Barbara Cartland

I feel so sorry for the young women of today because when they are old they will have no love-letters to revive nostalgic memories.

Telephones have swept away the thrill of recognizing the handwriting of a letter which has just arrived by post, and grooms on horseback no longer leave notes at the front door.

Herbert Asquith when he was Prime Minister wrote love-letters during Cabinet Meetings. The Marquess Curzon of Kedleston, an inveterate letter-writer, would sometimes write nineteen pages to the woman he loved.

But letters could also be a danger, an instrument of blackmail, and cause a lot of heartbreak.

The Honourable Henry Cust, the most fascinating ladykiller of the raffish Edwardians, was careless enough to allow the passionate love-letters he had received from the Marchioness of Londonderry to fall into the hands of the beautiful Countess de Gray.

Wildly jealous, she sent them to the Marquess. He read them, then enclosed them with a note to his wife:

"Henceforward we do not speak."

For thirty years the Londonderrys never addressed a single word to each other except those which were necessary during their appearances in public.

When her husband was dying the Marchioness sent him a note begging him to see her. The answer was "No!"

When the Marchioness lay dying the Countess sent her a telegram asking for forgiveness. The answer was "No!"

Aristocratic French lovers had their love-letters decorated by professional artists with cupids, pierced hearts, garlands of roses and arrows.

For me there is nothing more delightful and reassuring than to read of the love someone feels for me and to be able to treasure it.

"Everywhere I look I see your face and your eyes, the wind is the touch of your lips, the sun your smile."

"I love you until the whole world sings of my love."

"You're the most beautiful person I've ever seen. I can think and dream of nothing but you. If you won't marry me, I swear I'll kill myself!"

"Good morning, my darling, I want these roses to see you!"

"You have inspired me! If I am successful it is because you love me and believe in me and that is all that matters."

What telephone conversation can compete with that?

Lady Leslie said to her granddaughter:

"If ever you care for somebody write them a note every day - even if it is just one line."

For over forty years HRH Prince Arthur Duke of Connaught wrote to her.

When I was away from my husband he both telephoned and wrote to me without missing a single day.

Comte Roger de Bussy-Rabutin, an expert on love, advised lovers to write day and night because letters are "the fuel of love".

But young people ask: "What does one say in a love-letter? How does one write one?"

To answer these questions I have taken extracts from the letters of famous people.

All those which seemed to leap from the pages in a blaze of light were written with love.

Barbara Cartland

Ibn H'azm

The Andalusians, indolent, flamboyant and voluptuous, are the Romantics of Spain.

Ibn H'azm (tenth century), was one of the first of the great writers of love in Andalusia, and he collected poems and letters for his books. Many of these letters were of secret, sinful loves and had to be destroyed.

Abd-er-Rahman V complained of a fickle lady who had broken her promise to him:

> "Ah, weary are the nights since thou left me! O graceful gazelle, breaker of vows and faithless one, hast thou forgotten the hours we spent together on a bed of roses while the stars glittered above us like pearls in the blue vault of heaven?"

Ibn H'azm writes of his unhappiness over a young slave called Nu'm, whom he loved when he was young.

> "One could not dream of anything more desirable. She was perfect – physically and mentally. We understood each other. It was I who had had her virginity and we loved each other dearly. Destiny took her from me . . . when she died I was not yet twenty and she was even younger.
>
> For seven months after her death I did not take off my clothes and tears did not cease to fall from my eyes which as a rule do not moisten easily. I swear that I am still not consoled.
>
> If a ransom were possible I would buy her back with all my fortune. I would sacrifice a

member of my body. I have never tasted real happiness since she died; I have never forgotten her. I have never been satisfied in the intimacy of other women.

My love for her obliterated all my previous loves and rendered all that followed sacrilegious."

King Henry VIII

Henry VIII (1491-1547) to Lady Anne Boleyn - bewitching, vivacious, unscrupulous and irresistible - when he was waiting to be divorced from his first wife Catherine of Aragon:

King Henry VIII to Lady Anne Boleyn:

1528

" . . . No more to you at this present, mine own darling, for lack of time. But I would that you were in my arms, or I in yours - for I think it long since I kissed you.
Written after the killing of a hart, at eleven of the clock; purposing with God's grace, to-morrow, mighty timely, to kill another, by the hand which, I trust, shortly shall be yours.

HENRY R."

St François de Sales

A saint was born in the seventeenth century, the noble François de Sales (1567-1622). His mystic relationship with Ste Jeanne de Chantal is one of the greatest spiritual love stories of all time.

Both François and Jeanne had visions of each other in their dreams, and from the very beginning had a clear perception of the mysterious element in their relationship.

François wrote to Jeanne:

> "It seems to me that God has intended me for you and every hour I become more convinced of this. This is all I can say to you now. The farther I am from you in space the more strongly do I feel the link between us."

Later he wrote:

> "We both belong altogether to God, undividedly, unreservedly, with no craving save for the favour of being His. If we found in our hearts a single thread of love that did not come from Him and belong to Him, we would tear it out instantly.
>
> You must not any longer cling to human support; you must resign all you have had hitherto and cast yourself weak and desolate before God's mercy seat, remaining there stripped of everything and without a claim on any human sympathy in thought or act."

Jeanne replied:

"I rejoice that you should prolong your solitude, since you can still devote it to the needs of your soul. I say 'your', I may not say 'our' any longer, for I feel that I have no more share in it, so completely am I now deprived and shorn of everything I treasured most. How deep the knife has gone! to-day there seems nowhere for my soul to rest.

It is easy enough to give up outward comforts, but to give up one's skin and bone, to go down to the very marrow which it seems to me is what we have done, that is a tremendous thing, so hard as to be impossible without the grace of God.

Without your leave, I shall not seek for the happiness of intercourse with you . . . It seems as if I saw our souls united in entire resignation before God."

The Earl of Rochester

John Wilmot, 2nd Earl of Rochester (1647-1680), was the most outrageous of the Restoration rakes. He was also a lyrical and satirical poet. His witty satires and his erotic escapades amused Charles II, who forgave him his most embarrassing japes. When Rochester was in love with actress Mrs Barry he wrote to her:

The Earl of Rochester to Mrs Barry:

1674

"Since I am out of your presence (which is more intolerable to me than the sweetest death) I cannot live without a sight of you; so I wait your directions how I may once more be happy in the enjoyment of your company, which if you forbid me, you stick a dagger to my heart, which now bleeds for you."

Later he wrote:

"Madam, There is now no minute of my life that does not afford me some new argument how much I love you; . . .
   Lastly, the continual disquiet I am in, during your absence, convince me sufficiently that I do you justice in loving you, so as woman was never loved before."

John, Duke of Marlborough

From John, Duke of Marlborough (1650-1722) to Sarah Jennings, undated, covering a period of three years from 1675 to 1677:

The Wooing

"My Soul, I love you so truly well that I hope you will be so kind as to let me see you somewhere to-day, since you will not be at Whitehall. I will not name any time, for all hours are alike to me when you will bless me with your sight . . .

You are, and ever shall be, the dear object of my life, for by heavens, I will never love anybody but yourself."

* * *

"I beg that I may then have leave to see you tonight at eight, for believe me it is an age since I was with you . . .

I do love you so well that I have no patience when I have no hopes of seeing my dear angel, wherefore pray send me word that I shall be blessed and come at eight, till when, my Soul, I will do nothing else but think kindly of you."

Before leaving for the war Marlborough wrote:

"My Soul, I go with the heaviest heart that ever man did, for by all that is good I love you with all my heart and soul, and I am sure that as long as I live you shall have no just reason to believe the contrary . . .

If you are unkind, I love (you) so well that I cannot live, for you are my life, my Soul, my all that I hold dear in this world."

1677

Engaged

"It was unkind of you to go away last night since you knew that I came for no other purpose but to have the joy of seeing you, but I will not believe it was for want of love, for you are all goodness, the thought of which makes me love you above my own soul ..."

*   *   *

1677

"My heart is ready to break. I wish 'twere over, for since you are grown so indifferent, death is the only thing that can ease me."

Married

Jermyn Street,
1679

"... you may guess by yourself how uneasy I have been since I left you, for nothing breathing ever loved another so well as I do you, and I do swear to you as long as I live I will never love another; and if you do ever love me, I will always love you ..."

Edinburgh,
January 20th, 1680

"Although I believe you love me, yet you do not love so well as I, so that you cannot be truly sensible how much I desire to be with you.

I swear to you the first night I was blessed in having you in my arms was not more earnestly wished for by me than now I do to be again with you for if ever man loved woman truly well, I now do you.

For I swear to you were we not married I would beg you on my knees to be my wife, which I could not do did I not esteem you as well as I love you."

Sarah, Duchess of Marlborough, after John's death, to the Duke of Somerset when he wished to marry her:

"If I were young and handsome as I was, instead of old and faded as I am, and you could lay the empire of the world at my feet, you should never share the heart and hand that once belonged to John, Duke of Marlborough."

William Congreve

William Congreve (1670-1729), the great master of comedy, had many lady-loves. One of them was Mrs Arabella Hunt.

William Congreve to Mrs Arabella Hunt:

1690

"Not pretend that I love you? You cannot pretend to be so incredulous. Recall to mind what happened last night.

That at least was a lover's kiss. Its eagerness. its fierceness, and its melting softness expressed the God its parent. But Oh! its sweetness, and its melting softness expressed him more. With trembling in my limbs, and fevers in my soul I ravish'd it.

Convulsions, paintings, murmurings shew'd the mighty disorder within me: the mighty disorder increased by it.

For those dear lips shot through my heart, and thro' my bleeding vitals, delicious poison, and an avoidless but yet a charming ruin ..."

Madame Julie de Lespinasse

The Salons of eighteenth-century France had a special place of their own. Julie de Lespinasse, the natural daughter of the Cardinal de Tencin and Comtesse d'Alban, was so poor she was unable to offer her guests a meal, but the conversation sparkled.

Julie was charming, intelligent and passionate. Ste-Beuve said her love letters were like 'a torrent of lava!' She had two ardent lovers at the same time. One was the Marquis of Mora, son of the Spanish Ambassador in Paris. An impetuous young widower, he wrote her twenty-two letters in ten days.

The other was 29-year-old Colonel de Guibert. After Julie's death from an overdose of opium, their letters were discovered:

> "To live and to suffer - heaven, hell - that is what I want to feel. That is the climate I want to live in, not that temperate state in which the fools and automats by whom we are surrounded pass their time. I love to live, and I live to love ..."

> "I love you as one must love: excessively, to the point of madness and despair. There are two things which must never be mediocre: poetry and love ..."

> "Look upon me as a creature stricken by a fatal malady and treat me with all the care and gentleness that one bestows upon the dying ..."

> You are not worthy of the pain you cause me ... you do not deserve what I have suffered. *Adieu* - I love you wherever I am ..."

Catherine the Great

Catherine the Great of Russia (1729-1796) had many lovers. One of the most important was Prince Gregory Potemkin. Potemkin wrote a song to her in which one verse of the lyric ran:

> "Cruel gods!
> Why did you give her such charms
> And then exalt her so high?
> So far beyond reach of my arms
> Why give me this destiny?
> To love her, and her alone.
> Her whose sacred name ne'er my lips will part:
> Whose sacred image ne'er will leave my heart."

In 1774 Catherine wrote her love what she called "A Frank Confession". It was clearly a humble plea for love and in it she said:

> "The trouble is that my heart is loath to remain even one hour without love; it is said that human vices are often concealed under the cloak of kindness ...
>
> I ought not to write this to you, for you might stop loving me or refuse to go to the Army fearing that I should forget you, but I do not think I could do anything so foolish."

In the winter of 1774 they were secretly married at the Church of St Sampson in St Petersburg.

* * *

Catherine adored him: no other word will do. She who readily saw people in terms of animals gave

Potemkin a whole range of such endearments: Lion in the Jungle, Tiger, My Golden Pheasant, Dearest Pigeon, Little Parrot, Little Dog, Kitten. But also she called him Cossack, Giaour, Daddy, Twin Soul, Dearest Little Heart.

Even though she saw him almost continually, Catherine poured out her feelings in love-notes. Here is part of one of them:

> "There are few people with a will as strong as yours; few as handsome, intelligent and good company as you. I'm not at all surprised that you are said to have made so many conquests . . .
>
> How strange it is! The very things I've laughed at all my life have happened to me, even my being blinded by love for you. I cannot take my stupid eyes off you; I forget everything reason tells me and feel completely dazed when I'm with you.
>
> If I can I must avoid seeing you for at least three days in order to regain my senses; otherwise you will grow bored with me, and rightly so. I am very annoyed with myself today and have given myself a good scolding . . ."

Henry Frederick, Duke of Cumberland

Henry Frederick, Duke of Cumberland (1745-1790), was brother to George III and was known as a great lover. His most famous love-affair was with Henrietta Vernon, Lady Grosvenor, whose husband was unfaithful to her. He wrote to her:

Henry Frederick, Duke of Cumberland to Henrietta, Vernon, Lady Grosvenor:

17 - - ?

"My own dearest Love ...

I wish I dare lye all the while by your bed and nurse you - for you will have nobody near you that loves you as I do thou dearest Angel of my Soul o' that I could but bear your pain for you I should be happy ...

I am sure my angel is not in greater pain than what my heart feels for my adorable angel ...

Adieu God bless you and I hope before morning your dear little one."

Henry Frederick, Duke of Cumberland to Henrietta, Lady Grosvenor:

Written at Sea

"My dear little Angel,

Got to bed about 10 - I then prayed for you *my dearest love kissed your dearest little hair* and laye down and dreamt of you had you on the dear little *couch* ten thousand times in my arms kissing you and telling you how much I

24

loved and adored you and you seemed pleased but alas when I woke it found it all delusion *nobody by me but myself at sea* ...

I need not tell you I have had nothing in my thoughts but your dearself and long for the time to come back again to you will all the while take care of myself because you desire *my dear little Friend* ...

Does the angel of my heart pray do you take care of your dearself for the sake of your faithful servant who lives but to love you to adore you, and to bless the moment that has made you generous enough to own it to him I hope my dear nay I will dare to say you never will have reason to repent it ...

God bless you most amiable and dearest little creature living ..."

Emma Hamilton

Emma Hamilton (1761-1815), one of the most beautiful women in the world, was the daughter of a blacksmith. She was educated by Charles Greville when she was his mistress.

When he was bored with her he sent her to his Uncle, Sir William Hamilton, in Naples, who married her in 1791. She met Admiral Nelson in 1793, and theirs became one of the greatest love-stories of all time.

Emma Hart to Charles Greville:

Naples, 1st of August, 1786

". . . You have made me love you, made me good, you have abandoned me and some violent end shall finish our connection if it is to finish, but, Oh Greville, you cannot, you must not give me up, you have not the heart to do it . . .

You love me I am sure and I am willing to do everything in my power that you shall require of me and what will you have more and I only say this the last time, I will either beg or pray, do as you like . . ."

Lord Nelson to Lady Hamilton:

February 8th, 1801

"I do not think I ever was so miserable as this moment. I own I sometimes fear that you will not be so true to me as I am to you, yet I cannot, will not believe you can be false.

No, I judge you by myself; I hope to be dead before that should happen, but it will not. Forgive me, Emma, oh, forgive your own dear, disinterested Nelson.''

Nelson is madly jealous of the Prince Regent.

Lord Nelson to Lady Hamilton:

February 17th, 1801

"I am so agitated that I can write nothing, I knew it would be so, and you can't help it. Why did you not tell Sir William? Your character will be gone. Good God! he will be next to you, and telling you soft things. If he does, tell it out at table, and turn him out of the house.

Do not sit long. If you sing a song, I know you cannot help it, do not let him sit next to you, but at dinner he will hob glasses with you. I cannot write to Sir Wm, but he ought to go to the Prince and not suffer your character to be ruined by him . . .

He will put his foot near you. I pity you from my soul, as I feel confident you wish him in hell. Have plenty of people and do not say a word you can help to him. He wishes, I dare say, to have you alone.

Don't let him touch, nor yet sit next to you; if he comes, get up. God strike him blind if he looks at you - this is high treason, and you may get me hanged by revealing it. Oh, God, that I were.

I have read your letter, your resolution never to go where the fellow is, but you must have him at home. Oh, God! but you cannot, I suppose, help it, and you cannot turn him out of your own house . . .

I am more dead than alive, to the last breath yours. If you cannot get rid of this.

I hope you will tell Sir William never to bring the fellow again . . .

My longing for you, both person and conversation, you may readily imagine. What must be my sensations at the idea of sleeping with you! it setts me on fire, even the thoughts, much more would be the reality.

I am sure my love and desires are all to you, and if any woman naked were to come to me, even as I am this moment from thinking of you, I hope it might rot off if I would touch her even with my hand.

No, my heart, person, and mind is in perfect union of love towards my own dear, beloved Emma."

Lord Nelson to Lady Hamilton:

September, 1801

"I came on board, but no Emma. No, no, my heart will break. I am in silent distraction. The four pictures of Lady Hn are hung up, but alas! I have lost the original. But we part only to meet very soon again; it must be, it shall be . . .

My dearest wife, how can I bear our separation? Good God, what a change! I am so low that I cannot hold up my head . . .

When I reflect on the many happy scenes we have passed together, the being separated is terrible, but better times will come, shall come, if it pleases God."

Lord Nelson to Lady Hamilton:

Victory, October 19th, 1805

"My dearest beloved Emma, the dear friend of
my bosom,

The signal has been made that the Enemy's
Combined Fleet are coming out of Port. We
have very little wind, so that I have no hopes of
seeing them before tomorrow. May the God of
Battles crown my endeavours with success; at
all events, I will take care that my name shall
ever be most dear to you and Horatia, both of
whom I love as much as my own life.

And as my last writing before the Battle will
be to you, so I hope in God that I shall live to
finish my letter after the Battle. May Heaven
bless you prays your

NELSON AND BRONTE."

Two days later Nelson was mortally wounded.

Jean Paul Richter

Johann Paul Friedrich Richter (1763-1825), usually called Jean Paul, was a most important German humorist and according to Stefan George "the greatest German poetic power (although not the greatest poet)". He fell in love with Karoline von Feuchtersleben and she with him. Unfortunately they "fell out" by the end of the year.

Karoline to Richter:

Hildburghausen, Jan 31, 1800

"Dearest! I am yours! Oh! receive my soul and love me for ever and ever, as I do you! An hour ago came the dear, longed-for letters, which determine our life's happiness. Thank you, oh dearest one, a thousand thanks for your consideration, for your kindness and your love! ...

Oh, my beloved Richter, we shall be most happy together! God bless us both! I esteem and love you unutterably and will make you as happy as possible through my love. I cannot write, soon you will hear all about me and my hopes ...

Farewell and be joyful and happy as is

Your Karoline."

Karoline to Richter:

"Oh, beloved one! Everything is ringing in my head so loudly and joyfully. Waking this morning, I dreamt again the beautiful dream.

Ah! if only I were with you, I could take care of you so today! You angel, dear, only loved one! I cling to your breast, dearest, love always and always.

Your Karoline.''

Frederick, Duke of York

Frederick, Duke of York (1763-1827), was the second son of George III. In 1803 his mistress was Mary Anne Clarke, wife of a stonemason whom she deserted.

Frederick, Duke of York to Mrs Mary Anne Clarke:

Standgate, August 24th, 1804

"How can I sufficiently express to my darling love my thanks for her dear, dear letter or the delight which the assurances of her love give me? Oh my angel! do me justice and be convinced that there never was a woman adored as you are.

Every day, every hour convinces more and more that my whole happiness depends upon you alone. What a time it appears to be since we parted and with what impatience do I look forward to the day after to-morrow.

There are, still however, two whole nights before I shall clasp my darling in my arms ...!

Adieu, therefore, my sweetest, dearest love, till the day after to-morrow, and be assured that to my last hour I shall remain yours and yours alone."

The Empress Josephine

On 9 February 1796 the engagement between Josephine (1763-1814), widow of Alexander de Beauharnais was announced to General Napoleon Bonaparte (1769-1821).

For some time before this they had slept together and Napoleon wrote to her after their first night of love:

Napoleon Bonaparte to Josephine Beauharnais:

February, 1796
Seven o'clock in the morning

"My waking thoughts are all of you. Your portrait and the remembrance of last night's delirium have robbed my sense of repose. Sweet and incomparable Josephine, what an extraordinary influence you have over my heart. Are you vexed? Do I see you sad? Are you ill at ease? My soul is broken with grief and there is no rest for your lover . . .

But is there more for me when, delivering ourselves up to the deep feelings which master me, I breathe out upon your lips, upon your heart, a flame which burns me up? Ah! it was this past night I realised that your portrait was not you.

You start at noon. I shall see you in three hours. Meanwhile, *mio dolce amor*, accept a thousand kisses, but give me none, for they fire my blood."

After they were married it was not long before he was writing:

Napoleon to Josephine:

May, 1796?

"My life is a perpetual night mare, a presentiment of ill oppresses me. I see you no longer. I have lost more than life, more than happiness, more than my rest. I am almost without hope."

Napoleon to Josephine:

June, 1796

"A thousand kisses on your eyes, your lips, your tongue, your heart. Most charming of your sex, what is your power over me? I am very ill of your illness; I have still a burning fever. Do not keep the courier more than six hours, and let him return at once to bring me the longed for letter of my beloved."

On 20 June 1796 he wrote:

Napoleon to Josephine:

Bologna
June 20th, 1796

"I warn you that you have made me miserable. Cruel one, why have you left me to place hope in a feeling that you do not possess? . . . Every day death gallops around me. Is life worth making so much fuss about?

Adieu, Josephine. Remain in Paris. Do not write me any more. But at least respect my heath. A thousand daggers tear my soul; do

34

not drive them in any further. *Adieu*, my happiness, my love, everything that existed for me on earth!

'Bonaparte' "

A storm broke when Josephine was in Milan engrossed with her lover, Hippolyte Charles. Napoleon was jealous.

Napoleon to Josephine:

November, 1796?

"What inclination stifles and alienates love, the affectionate and unvarying love which you promised me? Who may this paragon be, this new lover, who engrosses all your time, is master of your days and prevents you concerning yourself about your husband?
Josephine, be vigilant; one fine night the doors will be broken in and I shall be before you."

Josephine and Charles fled to Genoa. Napoleon's letter followed her.

Napoleon to Josephine:

November 28th, 1796

"When I sacrifice all my desires, all my thoughts, every moment of my life, I obey the sway which your charms, your disposition, and your whole personality have so effectively exerted over my unfortunate heart.
I was wrong, since nature has not given me

attractions with which to captivate you, but what I do deserve from Josephine is her regard and esteem, for I love her frantically and uniquely.

Farewell, beloved wife; farewell, my Josephine. May Fate concentrate in my breast all the griefs and trouble, but may it give Josephine happy and prosperous days. Who deserves them more?

When it shall be quite settled that she can love me no more, I will hide my profound grief, and will content myself with the power of being useful and serviceable to her.

I reopen my letter to give you a kiss. Ah, Josephine . . . Josephine! . . .!''

When Napoleon was at the Castle of Finckenstein with the beautiful, golden-haired, 20-year-old Marie Walewski, who had abandoned her 70-year-old husband, he wrote to Josephine:

Napoleon to Josephine:

Castle of Finckenstein
May 10th, 1807

"I have just received your letter. I know not what you tell me about ladies in correspondence with me. . . . I love only my little Josephine, sweet, pouting, and capricious, who can quarrel with grace, as she does everything else, for she is always lovable, except when she is jealous; then she becomes a regular little devil.''

Napoleon had won. He had Europe at his feet, and now he wanted a divorce. He wrote:

36

Napoleon to Josephine:

Nymphenburg
October 21st, 1809

"I look forward with pleasure to seeing you
again, and I await that moment impatiently.
I send you a kiss.

Yours ever,
NAPOLEON."

It was the last he would ever send.

Prince Augustus

Prince Augustus (1773-1843) was the sixth son of George III. When he was twenty he fell in love in Rome with Lady Augusta Murray, who was six years older than he was.

They were married in 1793 by a Mr Gunn, an English clergyman, but the Court of Arches later declared the marriage illegal under the conditions of the Royal Marriage Act and the King cruelly separated them so that they did not see each other for six years.

Prince Augustus to Lady Augusta Murray:

4th April, 1793

"Will you allow me to come this evening? It is my only hope. Oh! Let me come, and we will send for Mr. Gunn. Everything but this is hateful to me. More than forty-eight hours have I passed without the slightest nourishment. Oh, let me not live so.

If Gunn will not marry me I will die ... I will be conducted in everything by you; but I must be married, or die. I would rather see none of my family than be deprived of you ...

Good God! What will become of me? I shall go mad, most undoubtedly."

Lady Augusta Murray to Prince Augustus:

April, 1793

"My treasure, my dearest life and love, how can I refuse you? And yet dare I trust to the happiness your letters promised me? You shall

come if you wish it. You shall do as you like;
my whole soul rejoices in the assurances of
your love, and to your exertions I will trust . . .

No one will ever be dearer to me, more
mine, than that of my Augustus, my lover, my
all.''

Jane Digby

Jane Digby (1777-1860), the greatest beauty of her day, irresistible, fascinating and reckless, married first Lord Ellenborough, from whom she ran away with Prince Schwarzenberg. She married twice more, had two Kings as lovers, and her fourth husband was Sheikh Abdul Medjuel el Mesrab, a Bedouin, the great love of her life. She was Queen of his tribe and her marriage with him was wildly, ecstatically passionate.

Her second husband, Baron Karl von Venningen, wrote to her an astonishing but unique letter after she had left him for Count Theotoky.

Karl von Venningen to Madame Theotoky:

1840

"*Chère amie*,

When you receive these lines, I shall be far away from Paris. But my last word must be for you, to tell you once more that which I told you so many times in person - that my friendship and my attachment to you will end only with my life, and that each time I shall have to prove it to you will be a source of great satisfaction to me.

May you find in those faraway lands where you will live the happiness I tried in vain to give you and which I regret so deeply is now forever lost to me.

It is the only true happiness, the kind which lasts until the grave - of this I am convinced. May God give it to you. This is the only thought which in part, with time - and *perhaps* - will console me in my own misfortune.

May I learn someday soon that you are completely happy. Think then, under that beautiful sky of the Orient, that in cold and sad Germany a warm and faithful heart is beating for you, a heart which will *never* forget the happiness and the heavenly bliss you gave him during several years.

If the Almighty should decide otherwise about our fate, remember me still – my house will be a secure haven for an unhappy Jane.

Again farewell, my dear one. When I have seen the children to whom I shall give your love and your gifts, I shall let you hear from me again. Write me soon and tell me your final plans.

Everything always to you,
Karl."

After Jane married Medjuel she loved him so much that when he was away for eighteen days she poured her tortured feelings into her journal:

"How much is my grief enhanced by the sad thought that I was not very kind to him sometimes!

Not attentive enough to his wishes in *little* things, such as not keeping his hours, not washing his hair when he wished it, stingy in little trifles, sometimes irritable and impatient and he is so kind and patient with me!

Oh, what would I not now give to see him! And when will this be granted? When? Oh when? Oh, if ever granted that I see him again how differently (with the grace of God) will I behave to him I so really love."

41

On another occasion when he was away she was distraught with jealousy. Then she received a letter from him.

"A letter from Medjuel! Oh what a moment! And that he was coming in a few hours. I nearly fainted. Then rose, mounted the Saklowyeh (a thoroughbred Arab mare), and rode to the dear Ras el Ain to meet him, the adored, the lost one!

Oh God, what shall I render thee for all thy benefits! Oh what a moment of joy was our meeting! What ecstasies of unreserved happiness!

We walked together to the Ras el Ain. Oh, what sweet explanations and doing away with all doubts and jealous fears!"

William Hazlitt

William Hazlitt (1778-1830), writer, journalist, lecturer and dramatic critic, fell in love with Sarah, a lodging-house girl, who sat on his knee and left him for a young man of her own class and mentality.

"I tore the locket which contained her hair (and which I used to wear continually in my bosom as the precious token of her dear regard) from my neck and trampled it in pieces. I could not stay in the room - I could not leave it - my rage, my despair were uncontrollable.

I shrieked curses on her name and on her false love, and the scream I uttered (so pitiful and so piercing was it that the sound of it terrified me) instantly brought the whole house house father, mother, lodgers and all, into the room. They thought I was destroying her and myself ...

I gathered up the fragments of the locket of her hair which were strewed about the floor, kissed them, folded them up in a sheet of paper and sent them to her with these lines written in pencil on the outside:

'Pieces of a broken heart, to be kept in remembrance of the unhappy. Farewell.'

I was stung with scorpions - my flesh crawled: I was choked with rage. She started up on her own likeness, a servant in place of a woman. She had fascinated, she had stung me and had returned to her proper shape, gliding from me after inflicting the mortal wound and instilling deadly poison into every pore; but her form lost none of its original brightness by the change of character but was all glittering, beauteous, voluptuous grace.

Seed of the serpent or of the woman, she was divine! I was transformed too, no longer human – my blood was of molten lead, my thoughts on fire ..."

Stendhal

Marie-Henri Beyle (1783-1842) is better known as Stendhal. A romantic, his success as a writer was because he was "the link which joins the modern novel to the novel of the eighteenth century."

He was in love with his mother and his whole emotional life was changed by her sudden and premature death. He wrote:

> "... I was in love with my mother ... I wanted to cover my mother with kisses and
> I wanted there not to be any clothes. She loved me passionately and often kissed me, and I returned her kisses with such fervour that she was often obliged to move away. I abhorred my father when he came and interrupted our kisses. I always wanted to kiss her on her breast. I lost her in childbirth when I was seven years old."

In 1818 in Milan he fell overwhelmingly in love with Metilde Dembowski. The day before his departure he wrote to her:

Stendhal to Metilde:

1818

> "I am very unhappy. I seem to love you more every day and you no longer feel for me the simple friendship which you used to show.
> There is a very striking proof of my love, and that is my awkwardness when I am with you. It makes me angry with myself, and I cannot overcome it. I am brave until I reach your Salon, and the moment I catch sight of you, I

45

tremble. I assure you that no other woman has inspired me with this feeling for a long while. It makes me so unhappy that I should like to be compelled not to see you any more . . .

I am leaving tomorrow, I am going to try to forget you if I can . . ."

Stendhal to Metilde:

"I love you much more when I am far away from you than I do when I am in your presence. When I am far away, I see you indulgent and good to me; your presence destroys these sweet illusions."

Stendhal to Metilde:

June 7th, 1818

"You cast me into despair. You accuse me several times of lacking in delicacy, as if, from your lips, this accusation was unimportant . . . This unhappy need I have of seeing you impels me, dominates me and transports me. There are moments, on long solitary evenings, when I should be a murderer, If I had to murder to see you . . .

Love me if you will, divine Metilde, but, in the name of God, do not despise me. This torment is more than I can bear."

Stendhal to Metilde:

August, 1818

"Farewell, madame, be happy. I believe you cannot be happy unless you love. Be happy, even in loving someone other than myself."

On 14 October he set off again for Milan.

46

Harriette Wilson

Harriette Wilson (1786-1846) was the most famous 'Cyprian' of her time. Her lovers included the Duke of Argyle, Lord Worcester and the Duke of Wellington, but she fell in love with Lord Ponsonby.

He wrote asking to meet her, and to prepare herself she shut herself up to read "The Greeks for two whole days, the Romans six more, then Rousseau's Confession, Racine's tragedies and Boswell's Life of Johnson".

Her answer to his letter was:

> "For the last five months, I have scarcely lived but in your sight, and everything I have done or wished, or hoped, or thought about, has had a reference to you and your happiness. Now tell me what you wish.
>
> HARRIETTE."

His reply was:

> "I fancy, though we never met, that you and I are, in fact, acquainted, and understand each other perfectly. If I do not affect to disbelieve you, you will not say I am in vain; and when I tell you that we cannot meet immediately, owing to a very severe domestic calamity, you will not say I am cold. In the meantime will you write to me . . .?
>
> But my poor father is dying, and counts the minutes of my absence. I know he will have your prayers. At midnight, let us pray for him together. He has been suffering more than five months. *Adieu*, dear Harriette."

Harriette noted in her Memoirs:

> "My happiness, while that correspondence
> went on, was the purest, the most exalted, and
> the least allied to sensuality, of any I ever
> experienced in my life. Ponsonby, I conceived,
> was now mine, by right; mine by that firm
> courage which made me feel ready to endure
> any imaginable evil for his sake.
>
> I was morally certain that nothing in
> existence could love Lord Ponsonby, or could
> feel the might and majesty of his peculiarly
> intellectual beauty, as I did."

He wrote:

> "My beloved, my spirits and health fail me;
> they are worn out and exhausted with this close
> confinement. My poor father no longer suffers,
> or is scarcely sensible. My brother George will
> take my place by his bedside. Let us meet this
> evening, and you will console me. I shall go to
> you at nine."

Lord Byron

George Gordon, Lord Byron (1788-1824), was a poet and a hero who will never be forgotten in Greece. His handsome raffish looks, his brilliant poetry, his numerous love-affairs, made him irresistible to women.

Lady Caroline Lamb was crazily and most uncontrollably infatuated with him.

Lord Byron to Lady Caroline Lamb:

London
August, 1812

"My Dearest Caroline,
If tears which you saw and know I am not apt to shed - if the agitation in which I parted from you, - agitation which you must have perceived through the *whole* of this most *nervous* affair, did not commence until the moment of leaving you approached, - . . . .
I was and am yours freely and most entirely, to obey, to honour, love, - and fly with you when, where and how you yourself *might* and *may* determine."

He had a strange, passionate love for his half-sister, the Honourable Augusta Leigh.

Lord Byron to Augusta Leigh:

Ouchy
September 17th, 1816

"What a fool I was to marry - and *you* not very wise - my dear - we might have lived so single

and so happy - as old maids and bachelors; I
shall never find any one like you - nor you
(vain as it may seem) like me . . .

Had you been a Nun - and I a Monk - that
we might have talked through a grate instead of
across the sea - no matter - my voice and my
heart are

ever thine - B."

To Countess Guiccioli, aged twenty, whom Byron
described as being "fair as sunrise, and warm as
noon - a sort of Italian Caroline Lamb, except she is
much prettier and not so savage," and he added: "I am
damnably in love."

Lord Byron to Countess Guiccioli:

Venice
25th April, 1819

"My love . . .
If you knew how great is the love I feel for
you, you would not believe me capable of
forgetting you for a single instant; you must
become better acquainted with me. Perhaps one
day you will know that, although I do not
deserve you, I do indeed love you . . .

Now I am all yours; I will become what you
wish - perhaps happy in your love, but never at
peace again . . .

You have been mine - and whatever the
outcome - I am, and eternally shall be entirely
yours. I kiss you a thousand and a thousand
times.

This unheaded and unsigned letter is assumed to
be written to the Honourable Augusta Leigh:

Venice
May 17th, 1819

"My Dearest Love . . .

I have never ceased nor can cease to feel for a moment that perfect and boundless attachment which bound and binds me to you - which renders me utterly incapable of *real* love for any other human being - for what could they be to me after *you*?

My own xxx* we may have been very wrong - but I repent of nothing except that cursed marriage - and your refusing to continue to love me as you had loved me - I can neither forget nor *quite forgive* you for that precious piece of reformation. - but I can never be other than I have been - and whenever I love anything it is because it reminds me in some way of yourself . . ."

* as he wrote it.

Lord Byron to the Countess Guiccioli:

Bologna
August 25th, 1819

"My dear Teresa, . . .

My destiny rests with you, and you are a woman, seventeen years of age, and two out of a convent. I wish that you had stayed there, with all my heart, - or, at least, that I had never met you in your married state.

But all this is too late. I love you, and you love me, - at least, you *say so*, and *act* as if you *did* so, which last is a great consolation in all events. But *I* more than love you, and cannot cease to love you.

Think of me sometimes, when the Alps and the ocean divide us, - but they never will, unless you *wish* it.

Byron."

Lord Byron to the Honourable Augusta Leigh:

Ravenna
September 7th, 1820

"My Dearest Augusta,
I always loved you better than any earthly existence, and I always shall unless I go mad . . .

Yours ever and truly,
Byron."

John Keats

John Keats (1795-1821) was one of those great poets, together with Shelley and Byron, of the English Romantics.

His short life was one of fiery love and burning beauty. When he fell in love with Fanny Brawne in 1818 he was swept into an ecstatic rapture. He wrote to her:

John Keats to Fanny Brawne:

October, 1819

"My love has made me selfish. I cannot exist without you. I am forgetful of everything but seeing you again. My Life seems to stop there - I see no further. You have absorb'd me. I have a sensation at the present moment as though I was dissolving.

I have been astonished that men could die martyrs for religion - I have shuddered at it. I shudder no more - I could be martyred for my religion - Love is my religion - I could die for that, I could die for you. My creed is Love and you are its only tenet."

Jane Carlyle

Jane Carlyle (1801-1866), formerly Jane Welsh, married Thomas Carlyle, author of *The French Revolution*. They were desperately poor, and their marriage was most successful when they were apart.

Jane Carlyle to Thomas Carlyle:

Craigenputtock
Templand
December 30th, 1828

"Goody, Goody, dear Goody,
You said you would weary and I do hope in my heart you are wearying. It will be so sweet to make it all up to you in kisses when I return. You will *take me* and hear all my bits of experiences, and your heart will beat when you find how I have longed to return to you ...
Darling, Dearest, Loveliest, 'The Lord bless you'. I think of you every hour, every moment. I love you and admire you, like - like anything. My own Good Good!
Good night, my beloved. Dream of me.
I am ever
Your own
GOODY."

George Sand

George Sand (1804-1876) had many lovers but she felt
more deeply for the poet Alfred de Musset than any of
them, except perhaps Chopin. She fell in love with
him in 1834 when she was thirty and he was twenty-
four.

George Sand to Chopin:

15th-17th April, 1834

"... Never, never believe Alfred, that I could be
happy if I thought I had lost your heart.
Whether I have been mistress or mother to you,
what does that matter? Whether I have inspired
you by love or by friendship, whether I have
been happy or unhappy with you - nothing of
this affects the present state of my mind. I know
that I love you, that is all ...
   When these atrocious memories besiege me
(and at what hour do they leave me in peace?) I
go nearly mad, I soak my pillow with tears: I
hear in the silence of the night your voice
calling me ...
   Oh, my child, my child! How much I need
your tenderness and your forgiveness! ..."

George Sand to Chopin:

Venice
12th May, 1834

"No, my sweet darling, those three letters are
not the last hand-clasp of the lover who is
quitting you ...

This feeling is too beautiful, too pure and too sweet for me ever to want to have done with it. Are you certain, you my sweet, of never being forced to shatter it? A new love, will it not impress this on you as a condition? May the remembrance of me not poison one of the joys of your life; but do not let those joys destroy and despise the remembrance of me. Be happy, be beloved. How should you not be so? . . .

For the first time in my life I love without passion.

You have not yet arrived at this yourself. Perhaps you are going in the opposite direction.

Perhaps your last love-affair will be the most romantic and the most youthful. But your kind heart, your kind heart - do not kill it, I pray you."

Elizabeth Barrett Moulton Barrett

Elizabeth Barrett Moulton Barrett (1806-1861) and Robert Browning (1812-1889) had the most romantic, dramatic love-story which will never be forgotten. They met, fell in love, eloped and wrote the most moving love-poems of all time. Their letters to each other are sheer poetry.

Robert Browning to Elizabeth Barrett Browning:

Wednesday
January 28th, 1846

"My only good in this world - that against which all the world goes for nothing - is to spend my life with you, and be yours.

Till tomorrow, and ever after, God bless my heart's own, own Ba. All my soul follows you, love - encircles you - and I live in being yours."

Elizabeth Barrett Browning to Robert Browning:

Friday
May 2nd, 1846

"I stand by a miracle in your love, and because I stand in it and it covers me, just for *that* you cannot see me! May God grant that you *never see me* - for then we too shall be 'happy' as you say, and I, in the only possible manner, be very sure ..."

Robert Browning to Elizabeth Barrett Browning:

Friday morning
April 10th, 1846

"*Now* kiss me, my best-dearest beloved! It seems I am always understood *so* - the words are words, and faulty, and inexpressive, or wrongly expressive, - but when I live under your eyes, and die, you will never mistake . . . dearest life of my life, light of my soul, heart's joy of my heart! . . .

Your own R."

Robert Browning to Elizabeth Barrett Browning:

Saturday
(Postmark May 2nd, 1846)

"I will look in the direction of London and send my heart there . . . Dear, dear love, I kiss you and commend you to God. Your very own - "

Elizabeth Barrett Browning to Robert Browning:

Wimpole Street
London

Friday Night
September 19th, 1846

"By tomorrow at this time, I shall have *you* only, to love me - my beloved!
You *only*! As if one said God *only*. And we shall have *Him* beside, I pray of him.

Is this my last letter to you, ever dearest?
Oh - if I loved you less . . . a little, little less.

Do you pray for me tonight, Robert? Pray for
me, and love me, that I may have courage
feeling both -

Your own
BA."

Fanny Kemble

Fanny Kemble (1809-1893) who, like members of her family, achieved fame as an actress, married and was also the darling of the *Beau Monde* during the Regency and reign of George IV.

She married a rich American, only to find he was a slave-owner. Her hatred of her husband's possessions in Georgia broke up the marriage, but even when relations between them were strained almost to breaking-point she could write to him:

Fanny Kemble to Pierce Butler:

1842

"Having never loved any human being as I have loved you, you can never be to me like any other human being, and it is utterly impossible that I should ever regard you with indifference . . .

My whole existence having once had you for its sole object . . . it is utterly impossible that I should ever forget this – that I should ever forget that you were once my lover and are my husband and the father of my children . . .

I cannot behold you without emotion, my heart still answers to your voice, my blood in my veins to your footsteps."

Queen Victoria

Queen Victoria (1819-1901) came to the throne in 1838. When her Ministers thought she should marry, they urged her to consider Prince Albert of Saxe-Coburg and Gotha. She was very reluctant. She might, she said, like him "as a friend . . . as a cousin and as a brother . . . but not more".

But when she stood at the top of the stairs at Windsor Castle to greet him upon his return to England, she immediately fell utterly in love with him.

After she had proposed to him she wrote:

> "He was so, so affectionate. Oh! to feel I was, and am, loved by *such* and Angel . . . He is *perfection*; perfection in every way - in beauty - in everything . . . Oh! How I adore and love him."

After their wedding on 10 February 1840, Victoria recorded in her Journal:

> "He was 'so dear and kind'. We had our dinner in our sitting room, but I had such a sick headache that I could eat nothing, and was obliged to lie down . . . for the remainder of the evening on the sofa - but ill or not, I NEVER, NEVER spent such an evening!
>
> My DEAREST DEAREST DEAR Albert sat on a footstool by my side, and his excessive affection gave me feelings of heavenly love and happiness I never could have hoped to have felt before!
>
> He clasped me in his arms, and we kissed each other again and again!

His beauty, his sweetness and gentleness -
really how can I ever be thankful enough to have
such a *Husband*! ... To be called by names of
tenderness I have never yet heard used to me
before - was bliss beyond belief!

Oh, this was the happiest day of my
life! - May God help me to do my duty as I
ought and be worthy of such blessings!''

Richard Burton

Richard Burton (1821-1891), one of the world's greatest travellers and finest Oriental scholars – he spoke twenty-seven languages – was the only European at the time to penetrate the forbidden City of Mecca.

Isobell Arundell, tall, strong, auburn-haired, wildly passionate, saw him, fell in love and was determined to marry him. It took her ten years.

When Richard proposed in 1856 Isobel wrote in her diary:

Isobel Arundell:

1856

"I would have suffered six years more for such a day. Such a moment as this. All past sorrow was forgotten in it. Men might as well undertake to describe Eternity. I then told him all about my six years since I first met him. And all that I suffered. When I got home I knelt down and prayed, and my whole soul flooded with joy and thanksgiving. I feel that I have at last met the master who can subdue me."

They have a three-year separation. Isobel, aged twenty-eight, pines and prays.

Isobel Arundell:

1859

"I love and am loved, and so strike a balance in favour of existence ...

Whatever harshness the future may bring, *he has loved me*, and my future is bound up in

him with all consequence. My jealous heart
spurns all compromise: it must have its
purpose or break ..."

Richard was searching for the greatest geographical
secret after the discovery of America: the source of the
Nile.

He sends a letter to Isobel from Zanzibar in 1859
which contains a single page.

Richard Burton to Isobel:

1859

TO ISOBEL

"That brow which rose before my sight,
As on the palmers' holy shrine;
Those eyes – my life was in their light,
Those lips my sacramental wine;
That voice whose flow was wont to seem
The music of an exile's dream."

Isobel's parents disapproved of the marriage and in
a very long letter to her mother she wrote:

Isobel Arundell to her mother:

"... The moment I saw his brigand-dare-devil
look I set him up as an idol and determined
that he was the only man I would ever marry ...
But when I came home one day in ecstasy and
told you that I had found the Man and the Life
I longed for, and that nothing would turn me,
and that all other men were his inferiors, what
did you answer me? That he was the *only* man
you would never consent to my marrying; that

you would rather see me in my coffin. Did you know that you were flying in the face of God? Did you know it was my destiny? . . . *I wish I were a man. If I were, I would be Richard Burton; but being only a woman, I would be Richard Burton's wife.*"

On 22 January 1861 Isobel married her King, her god, a wild-eyed leopard whom she tried to tame.

Sarah Bernhardt

Sarah Bernhardt (1845-1923) was in her prime known as "the Eighth Wonder of the World", and even in her declining years was the greatest actress and personality France had produced since Joan of Arc. She had Emperors kneeling at her feet, Kings showering her with jewels, admiring crowds throwing their coats on to the ground for her to walk on.

In 1887 when she was forty-three, a young man, Pierre Loüys, who was later to gain literary fame, saw her in *La Tosca* and wrote in his diary:

Pierre Loüys:

> "Oh! Sarah! Sarah! Sarah is grace! Sarah is youth! Sarah is beauty! Sarah is divinity!
>
> I am mad, I am beside myself! I no longer know what I'm doing. I no longer think of anything. I saw Sarah Bernhardt last night.
>
> My God! What a woman! Sarah ... Sarah ... when shall I see you again? I weep, I tremble, I grow mad, Sarah I love you!"

George Bernard Shaw

George Bernard Shaw (1856-1950), an intellectual giant, and Mrs Patrick Campbell (1865-1940), the great and beautiful actress whose brilliant personality dominated the English-speaking stage for fifty years, fell in love.

Their letters began in 1899 when Shaw was forty-two and Mrs Campbell thirty-four, and ended when he was eighty-three and she was seventy-four, within a year of her death.

Beatrice Campbell to George Bernard Shaw:

33, Kensington Square
1st November, 1912

". . . Oh darling! I think DD and I behaved like ungrateful savages, and you so good, and so gentle with us - and so kind to come and see me at all and honour me by reading your *brilliant* play -

- Oh dear me - it's too late to do anything but accept you and love you - but when you were quite a little boy somebody ought to have said 'hush' just once!

Grateful,
Beatrice."

George Bernard Shaw to "Stella", Beatrice Campbell:

10, Adelphi Terrace, W.C.
8th November, 1912

"Stella, Stella,
Shut your ears tight against this blarneying Irish liar and actor. Read no more of his letters.

He will fill his fountain pen with your heart's blood, and sell your most sacred emotions on the stage ...

He is a mass of imagination with no heart, he is a writing and talking machine that has worked for nearly forty years until its skill is devilish ...

Oh, don't, don't, DON'T fall in love with him; but don't grudge him the joy he finds in being in love with you, and writing all sorts of wild but heartfelt exquisite lies – lies, lies, lies, lies to you, his adorest.

G.B.S.''

George Bernard Shaw to "Stella", Beatrice Campbell:

Ayot St. Lawrence
Welwyn
6th February, 1913

"Stella, Stella what is there left for me to say?

I have just played all sorts of things, almost accurately, I don't believe I could get a headache if I tried. I drove from Hatfield faster than a man should drive in the dark.

What an enormous meal of happiness! They will wish you many happy returns of Sunday. Sunday! I laugh hollowly. When I am dead let them put an inscription on 12 Hinde Street:

'HERE A GREAT MAN FOUND HAPPINESS.'

G.B.S.''

George Bernard Shaw to "Stella", Beatrice Campbell:

10, Adelphi Terrace, W.C.
27th February, 1913

"Cruel stony hearted wretch, snatcher of bread from a starving child, how had you the heart? how could you? do you know what it means to me? I want my plaything that I am to throw away. I want my Virgin Mother enthroned in heaven. I want my Italian peasant woman . . .

I want my rapscallionly fellow vagabond. I want my dark lady. I want my angel - I want my tempter. I want my Freia with her apples. I want the lighter of my seven lamps of beauty, honour, laughter, music, love, life and immortality . . .

I want my inspiration, my folly, my happiness, my divinity, my madness, my selfishness, my final sanity and sanctification, my transfiguration, my purification, my light across the sea, my palm across the desert, my garden of lovely flowers, my million nameless joys, my day's wage, my night's dream, my darling and my star . . .

O cruel, cruel, cruel, cruel, have you no heart at all?

G.B.S."

George Bernard Shaw to "Stella", Beatrice Campbell:

Kilteragh, Co. Dublin
3rd April, 1913

". . . So if you are idly curious as to whether I am still in love with Stella, the answer is yes yes yes yes yes yes yes yes yes yes yes yes yes yes yes

69

yes yes yes yes yes yes yes yes yes yes yes yes yes
yes and a million times yes . . .

Cannot help it. Am quite sensible, quite able,
quite myself, and yet a lad playing with you on
the mountains and unable to feel where you
begin and I leave off. And if you tell me that
you feel like that the sky will not be high
enough for me (isn't that a nice Irish phrase?)

Heavens! how delicious it is to make love to
you!!!!!

G.B.S."

"Stella", Beatrice Campbell to George Bernard Shaw:

33, Kensington Square, W.
5th January, 1914

"Such a wonderful beautiful letter. Where are
you? I will tell you how it was with me that
New Year's Eve.

If I could write letters like you, I would write
letters to God –

Stella."

Lady Sackville

Victoria Sackville-West (1862-1936) was the daughter of a British Diplomat and his Spanish gypsy mistress. She grew up in France badly educated, illegitimate and insecure. But when in 1881 her father was appointed Head of the British Legation in Washington she became his hostess.

Fascinating and beautiful, with an irresistible charm, she flirted with all the men who courted her.

One wrote to her:

> ". . . I tell you that you are charming, fascinating heaven knows what. There is no end to your perfections – but you have one great fault, I can neither forgive nor forget – simply that you like other people better than me . . . Your speciality is love, you are an accomplished mistress of that art; only it's not art, it's nature. You play with it and manage it, like a seagull the winds; on which he floats but which never carries him away . . ."

In England Victoria met her cousin Lionel Sackville-West, five years younger than herself. On 11 December 1889 he proposed to her in the King's Bedroom at Knole (the first Elizabethan house in England), and she accepted him.

They were married on 17 June 1890 in the Chapel at Knole. She received a telegram:

> *"Joie de ma vie* all of my love, Lionel."

Their honeymoon was one of sheer physical rapture. Wherever they stayed they went to bed immediately.

"Baby", which was Victoria's name for a certain part of Tio's (as she called Lionel) anatomy, was in "a chronic condition"!

Knole
31 July, 1890

"Tio has gone out again to kill deer. Miss Boscawen came to see us and told L. that he was looking badly. I told Tio that this was because of e.g! (making love)."

Knole
2 August, 1890

"Baby was very naughty this morning while I was pretending to sleep . . ."

20 August, 1890

"Tio is getting more passionate every day."

13 September, 1890

"Baby was very naughty this morning, we kept Mrs Knox waiting for forty minutes - awful of us."

16 September, 1890

"Tio got up even later than usual this morning; simply can't leave me and often returns about 11 o'clock so that we can have caresses that never end."

18 September, 1890

"Tio was perfectly mad tonight - he kissed me passionately even in front of Amalia and Bertie, which ended in the most delicious love-making. He really is a stallion - 4 times."

28 November, 1890

"Delirium. Afterwards Tio said: 'Was it nice, Vicky?'"

22 May, 1890 Knole

"Every day the same thing, walking and sticking stamps on, reading, playing the piano, making love."

27 June, 1890 Knole

"What a heavenly husband I have and how different our love and union is from that of other couples."

David Lloyd George

David Lloyd George (1863-1945), one of the greatest
political figures in England and Prime Minister
during the war; and his secretary, Frances Stevenson,
whom he called "Pussy", were lovers for over thirty
years.

Their passion and devotion to each other started in
February 1913, and after Dame Margaret Lloyd
George's death in 1943, they were married.

David Lloyd George to Frances Stevenson:

The House of Commons

"My darling little girl,
I am deeply grieved I spoke so sharply to you
this morning, and I apologise to you from the
bottom of a contrite and loving heart.

It was in addition to other faults a distinct
breach of faith after the promise I gave you not
to worry you.

Forgive me darling - because I love you with
an inexhaustible affection and tenderness and I
care not one jot for the past.

Ever your own
D."

David Lloyd George to Frances Stevenson:

Criccieth
8th August, 1915

"My own sweet little Pussy,
I am longing to be back with you. I am
becoming more intolerant of these partings

month by month. I cannot live now without my darling. I know that better even than I did weeks ago. It is either you or nothing for me *Cariad* ...

You are everything to me now. My failure or success will depend entirely on you. You possess my soul entirely ...

Oh I do want to see you - I want *you* and no one and nothing else.

Your own
D. - for ever."

David Lloyd George to Frances Stevenson:

Danny
Hassocks, Sussex
? early August, 1918

"Cariad Anwyl,

When I woke up at 6 my first thought was of the loving little face engraved on my heart and I had a fierce impulse to go there and then to cover it with kisses. But darling I am jealous once more ...

I know your thoughts are on roast mutton and partridge and chicken and potatoes and that you are longing to pass them through the lips which are wine and to bite them with luscious joy with the dazzling white teeth that I love to press.

I know that today I am a little out of it and that your heart is throbbing for other thrills ...

I shall bide my time feeling confident I will in the end beat the mutton chops and win back the delight of my fickle little *cariad* and it is worth waiting for.

Your very jealous old
Lover."

David Lloyd George to Frances Stevenson:

Danny
Hassocks, Sussex
August/September, 1918

"My darling,

This is to warn you at the earliest possible moment that I have once more fallen desperately in love with an *absolutely new girl*. She is the darlingest girl I ever met. I saw her for the first time yesterday afternoon lying (in the most seductive attitude) on a sofa.

She was attired in a love of a dressing-gown. She had the dearest face I ever saw - the most alluring smile - her neck was simply provoking. Altogether I am clean gone.

I hope one day to make her love me as much as if I were a grilled kidney swimming in fat.

Ever and Ever
Her
lover."

Frances Stevenson to David Lloyd George:

Paris
9th October, 1923

"My own darling, beloved little man,

I am so afraid that what you see over there will make you dissatisfied with what is over here, and that the charming people you are meeting may distract your love from me ...

No, I don't really think that - I know now that you do not change and that when you come back you will be just the same sweet lover, and perhaps with an added tenderness to meet

the increased tenderness I am feeling for you
after all your endeavours and achievements . . .

I have never loved you so much, or been so
happy in your love, as now, my darling, when
you are going through this ordeal. I am so
proud of my little man, so terribly proud.

P."

Laura Mary Octavia Lyttleton

Laura Mary Octavia Lyttleton (1863-1886) was born a Tennant, and was sister of the exuberant Margot. She was beautiful, and in her sister's words she "made and left a deeper impression on the world in her short life than anyone that I have ever known".

Laura married Alfred Lyttleton, the nephew of W. E. Gladstone, and died having a baby when she was twenty-three.

> *"My Will made by me, Laura Mary Octavia Lyttleton.*
>
> February, 1886

I have not much to leave behind me, should I die next month, having my treasure deep in my heart where no one can reach it, and where even Death cannot enter . . .

I want, first of all, to tell Alfred that all I have in the world and all I am and ever shall be, belongs to him, and to him more than anyone, so that if I leave away from him anything that speaks to him of a joy unknown to me, or that he holds dear for any reason wise or unwise, it is his, and my dear friends will forgive him and me. So few women have been as happy as I have been every hour since I married - so few have had such a wonderful sky of love for their common atmosphere, that perhaps it will seem strange when I write down that the sadness of Death and Parting is greatly lessened to me by the fact of my consciousness of the eternal, indivisible oneness of Alfred and me.

I feel as long as he is down here I must be here, silently, secretly sitting beside him as I do every evening now, however much my soul is the other side, and that if Alfred were to die, we would be as we were on earth, love as we did this year, only fuller, quicker, deeper than ever, with a purer passion and a wiser worship.

Only in the meantime, whilst my body is hid from him and my eyes cannot see him, let my trivial toys be his till the morning comes when nothing will matter because all is spirit ..."

Elinor Glyn

Elinor Glyn (1864-1942), the fiery, tempestuous red-haired beauty whose novel *Three Weeks* shocked and delighted the Edwardians, met George Nathaniel Curzon, 1st Marquess of Kedleston, and her feelings for him became a raging fire. In 1910, after staying with his family in the country, she wrote in her diary:

"O thou great one, calm and wise, accept this my cry of worship. Know that for me thou canst do no wrong. Thou are the mainspring of my life, for whom I would die, for whom I would change my character, curb my instincts, subjugate every wish, give my body and soul, worship blindly. Maimed or sick, well or strong, thou art adored, my arms for thy comfort, my soul for thy assuagement."

In 1916 Elinor Glyn had the first suspicions that their love-affair was drawing to a close and she wrote:

"Oh, I realise no man matters but my Lord, and I must crush all that and be a cynic and when I see you, oh my heart, I must be gay and not feel, and there is some change, I know it, in me. It is the third stage, it is of a tender place that is growing a hard surface to protect itself.
I am afraid of suffering but I must be gay, for of what good to be tortured? The moment might come when you would again think only of what was *best for you*, and then what would become of me? Should I die, or simply go to hell? ..."

A few months later she wrote:

> "But I love you, not *because* of your noble
> mind and your greatness, nor in *spite* of your
> selfishness, but just because I do, and you are
> you, for me the sun, moon and stars to the end
> of time."

On 11 December 1916 she opened *The Times* to read
that Curzon was engaged to Mrs Alfred Duggan.

Their passionate association had lasted for eight
and a half years, but he had not warned her of what he
intended to do. She never saw or wrote to him again.

He had written her five hundred letters. She burnt
them all - a funeral pyre of her greatest and last love.

HM King George V

George, Duke of York (1865-1936), was married on 6 July 1893 to Princess May of Teck, who was acutely shy, and the Duke, while highly emotional, found it hard to express what he felt.

They wrote passionately frank letters to each other, but found it difficult to break through their traditional Victorian reserve when they were face to face.

Some months after their wedding the Duke wrote:

George, Duke of York to Princess May of Teck:

York Cottage
Sandringham
1894

"You know by this time that I never do anything by halves, when I asked you to marry me I was very fond of you, but not very much in love with you, but I saw in *you* the person I was capable of loving most deeply, if you only returned that love . . .

I have tried to understand you and to know you, and with the happy result that I know now that I do *love* you, darling girl with all my heart, and am simply *devoted to you* . . .

I adore you sweet May.

George."

Princess Mary (she was called Mary after she married) replied to one of his letters:

"What a pity it is that you cannot *tell* me what you write, for I should appreciate it so enormously."

The Princess was to have married the Duke's elder brother, known as Eddy, but he died of pneumonia in June, 1892.

It was not a love-match, and although the Princess was deeply distressed she accepted Prince George the following year.

Their love grew until on becoming King in May, 1910 George wrote in his diary:

King George V:

> "God will help me in my great responsibilities and darling May will be my comfort as she has always been."

Tzar Nicholas II

Tzar Nicholas II (1868-1918) adored his wife
Alexandra, who - shy, retiring and German - was
hated by the people. She worshipped him and meant
well, although her friendship with Rasputin undoubtedly accelerated the revolution, when both the
Tzar, Tzarina and their children were all assassinated.

The Tzarina to the Tzar:

Tzarskoje Selo
December 5th, 1916

"My own Sweetheart,
  From the depths of my loving heart I send
you warmest, heartiest good wishes and many
tender blessings for yr. dear Namesday. May yr
patron saint quite particularly be near you and
keep you in safeguard. Everything that a
devoted, unuttterably loving heart can only
wish you - Sunny wishes you. Strength,
firmness, unwavering decision, calm, peace,
success, brightest sunshine - rest and happiness
at last after yr hard, hard fighting. In thought I
clasp you tightly to my heart, let your sweet,
weary head rest upon my breast . . .
  Now I must end. Sleep well and peacefully,
beloved Angel. The Holy Virgin guards you
and Gr. prays for you and we do all so hard.
  I cover you with tenderest, passionately
loving kisses and caresses and long to be of use
and help in carrying yr heavy Cross. God bless
and protect you, my Nicky. Every yr. very own

Wify."

The Tzarina to the Tzar:

"My own, my very own sweet One,
    I am so happy for you that you can at last manage to go, as I know how deeply you have been suffering all this time - yr. restless sleep even has been a proof of it . . .
    Egoistically I suffer horribly to be separated – we are not accustomed to it and I do so endlessly love my very own precious Boysy dear. Soon twenty years that I belong to you and what bliss it has been to be your very own little Wify! . . .
    I bless you and love you, as man was rarely loved before - and kiss every dearly beloved place and press you tenderly to my own heart.
    For ever yr. very own old

Wify."

The Tzarina to the Tzar:

Tzarskoje Selo
August 22nd, 1915

"My very own beloved One,
    I cannot find words to express all I want to - my heart is far too full. I only long to hold you tight in my arms and whisper words of intense love, courage, strength and endless blessings. More than hard to let you go alone, so completely alone - but God is very nice to you, more than ever . . .

I clasp you tenderly to my heart, kiss and caress you without end – want to show you all the intense love I have for you, warm, cheer, console, strengthen you and make you sure of yourself. Sleep well my Sunshine, Russia's Saviour. Remember last night, how tenderly we clung together. I shall yearn for yr. caresses - I never can have enough of them. And I still have the children and you are all alone. Another time I must give you Baby for a bit to cheer you up. -

I kiss you without end and bless you. Holy Angels guard your slumber - I am near and with you for ever and ever and none shall separate us. -

Yr very own wife
Sunny."

Mary, Lady Curzon

Mary Leiter (1870-1904) was an American born in the suburbs of Chicago. She became the wife of George Nathaniel Curzon, and Vicereine of India.

Daughter of a millionaire, she was gentle, sweet, compassionate, and she enriched her stiff, brilliant and difficult husband not only with money but with a love and joy.

In 1893 they became secretly engaged in Paris and Curzon wrote to her:

George Curzon to Mary Leiter:

Paris, 1893

"You very sweet last night, Mary, and I do not think I deserved such consideration. While I ask you, and while you consent, to wait, you must trust me, Mary, wholly, even as I would trust you, and all will be right in the end. I will not breathe a word to a human soul ...

Sometimes if you are down in your luck, you will remember that my kiss of love has rested upon your lips. God bless you, my darling child."

A year later when they had not seen each other he wrote:

George Curzon to Mary Leiter:

March 3rd, 1894

"Wide open and eager with delight will be the lover's arms into which (given a reasonable seclusion) you will spring, and already in anticipation are being formed the kisses that lips will leave on lips."

After a visit to Humza when he was in great danger Mary wrote to him in October the same year:

Mary Leiter to George Curzon:

October, 1894

"I can't speak for thankfulness. You are safe! You are safe! Safe for my love, and oh dear, I cannot write for joy. I have never had a moment of such transcendent thankfulness in all my life."

They were married in April, 1895. In March, 1901, when Curzon was Viceroy of India, Mary took her children to England for a six-month holiday.

The tedious journey from Bombay was relieved only by her daily letters to "Darling, darling Pappy", as she called her husband. Some of her letters were sixty-four pages long.

George Curzon to his wife:

1901

"Poor Pappy gets so downcast sometimes in all this whirl-wind of calumny and fiction . . .
   You don't know, or perhaps you do, what my isolation has been this summer. I am crying now so that I can scarcely see the page. But it has always been so. The willing horse is flogged till he drops, and the world goes on. Darling, your letters are my only solace."

Mary Curzon to her husband:

1901

"I want you, beloved Pappy, so desperately and rebel against this separation. I do love you - but what is the use of a loving woman 4,000 miles away from your arms?

I do feel in my heart that in our life there is a sense of comradeship almost as great as love.

In September, 1904, after two operations, Mary was dying. Curzon wrote of their last hours together:

"She was now perfectly tranquil and began to talk to me about our love and our life.

'Oh how happy we have been. You have been my only love. I have loved you intensely and you have made me utterly happy for ten years. We have done a great deal together, George. We have succeeded . . .'

Over and over she murmured: 'My darling, my sweet Pappy . . .'

She said our love letters have been wonderful and who that read them could doubt that ours had been a wonderful love. We talked of our marriage day, and of her look at me and mine at her as we stood side by side on the steps of the altar and the lovelights shone in her eyes . . .

As I left the room her last words were: 'My darling.'"

Mary (Polly) Cartland

Mary Cartland, my mother (1879-1976), pretty, small, vivacious, she was nicknamed 'Polly' because she talked so much.

She had the courage of her Scobell ancestors, the oldest Saxon family in existence, which carried her through a financial crisis when her father-in-law, an enormously rich financier lost all his money, the death in action of her husband in 1918, and the deaths of both her sons at Dunkirk.

She helped and inspired everyone who knew her.

After a three-week visit to Scotland when she was seventeen, she received a letter from a Scottish admirer:

Forfar, Scotland
1896

"Everything reminds me of you so much. If I go into the drawing-room, the piano reminds me of you and your violin and the 'Shepherds' Dance', and 'One More', and I feel miserable. Then if I go into the dining-room, there's somebody missing from the table and I'm miserable . . .

Everything reminds me of those three sweet sweet weeks when every day you did some kind thing I can never forget. Darling little Polly, I miss you every minute and love you more than ever.

I've got your dear photograph in front of me. You are far, far prettier than that, but don't think that is why I love you – it's your dear, sweet, good heart that I love most – a heart as good as gold."

From another young man she met during the same visit who wanted to marry her, but had no money. He loved her all his life.

"... darling, how I love you! You seem to me to be so absolutely perfectly lovely that I am sometimes staggered how you can bother your head about me.

I thought last night I might be able to drown myself in sleep. But divil a bit, fearfully restless with a sort of feeling of regret and pain - up and down my room I had to walk like a caged animal, and indeed I'm no better in the daytime.

I wrote two letters last night to you and burnt them both. I'm shivering so that I can't write ...

How I long to see you and gaze into your sweet eyes which have the power to make me drunk with love!"

Polly became engaged to Bertram Cartland in 1900. The Boer War had started and he wrote to her on his way to Aldershot:

Bertie to Polly:

1900

"My Darling, ...

Oh, my love, it is heaven when I am with you and hell, simply hell, when I am away.

One never realises till one is apart. Oh, darling, you know how I love you, don't you? ...

I know, my love, I am marrying a girl miles, *miles* too good for me and one who will stick to

me through thick and thin. Why I have such
luck as to have you, my darling, I don't know;
but oh, my love, I will do all in my power to
make you happy.

You are everything in the wide, wide world
to me, more than Father, Mother and even
honour, I think.

God bless you, darling,
Bertie.''

War was declared on 4 August 1914. Bertie was on
the Reserve and left with the Worcestershire Yeomanry
for Plymouth.

Bertie to Polly:

"My Darling,
Just a line before post. I loved seeing you, my
dearest. There has never been anyone in the
world for me but you, and you alone can do
everything for me . . .

I felt so miserable when I left. Take care of
yourself. Darling, I love you. God bless you.

Your own Bertie.''

Bertie was sent out to France with his Regiment and
wrote:

Bertie to Polly:

1914

". . . I write to you every day, my own dear
darling. I love and long for you always.

Your own Bertie.''

After three years in the trenches Bertie wrote:

Bertie to Polly:

June 6th, 1917

"My Own Darling,
    We go back into the line again to-morrow
night . . .
    All my dear, dear love, my own darling . . . I
do *so* long to get to you.

Yours as always,
Bertie."

The Worcesters were moved into a supporting
position near Messines.

Bertie to Polly:

June 15th, 1917

"Good-bye, angel mine. I will write whenever I
get the chance. I am glad I know you pray for
me - there is nothing like it in the world. All
my love, angel.
    Don't forget me although I am so far and so
long away. I love you more than anything on
earth."

The casualty lists grew longer and larger, but Bertie
seemed to have a charmed life.

Bertie to Polly:

June 21st, 1917

". . . No news, darling mine. I am certain it is
your prayers that bring me all the luck I have
had. All my love, angel. I long to see you,
darling.

Always your own Bertie."

After three months' sick-leave Bertie returned to France. He was not really fit, but he insisted on returning because his sense of duty demanded it. This time he was on the Cambrai front.

Bertie to Polly:

November 10th, 1917

"My Own Darling . . .
 Darling, I have so loved our time together and, oh my love, I do so hate leaving my own dear wife. I will try and do all you want, and if I succeed it will be entirely due to my having the best wife in all the world.
 Darling, so many things I wanted to say to you but never did. I am bad at telling you how much I love you, but you *do* know, don't you?
 I suppose it is right to do one's bit; but it is hard, and now I am getting old I grudge every moment away from your side. All my love, my own darling - my own dear wife.

Your own Bertie."

The Germans with their unfailing faculty for discovering a weak spot had, unknown to the Allies, moved three thousand guns into position to support a concentrated attack which was fixed for 1 a.m. on 27 May. It was the last phase in the great gamble for victory.

Bertie to Polly:

May 26th, 1918

"My Own Darling,
 Got your letter late last night. Thank you, dear, for your good wishes. Yes, 42 is old, and I

feel it at times. Poured with rain all the morning and the trenches are in a beastly state . . .

As I write the Hun is just starting to shell but not too heavily.

All my love, angel mine. God bless you and keep you, darling.

> *Dear* love, ever your own
> Bertie.''

Everywhere companies and platoons made a fierce and gallant resistance. One by one they were overwhelmed. There was no surrender. All fought to the last.

James Joyce

James Joyce (1882-1941), one of the greatest novelists of our era, a genius obsessed by women and drink, who ranged in his life and his writing from high spiritually to low, vulgar, obscene sensuality.

He fell wildly in love with Nora Barnacle, whom he subsequently married. He wrote:

James Joyce:

1909

> "Her soul! Her name! Her eyes! They seem to me like strange beautiful blue wild-flowers growing in some tangled, rain-drenched hedge. And I have felt her soul tremble beside mine, and have spoken her name softly to the night, and have wept to see the beauty of the world passing like a dream behind her eyes."

Clementine Churchill

Clementine Churchill (1885-1977) was beautiful, fascinating and intelligent. She married Sir Winston Churchill, the greatest man of the century, whose personality and charm were unassailable. Theirs was one of the world's greatest love stories.

Engaged

Winston Churchill to Clementine:

Blenheim Palace
August, 1908

"... The purpose of this letter is to send you heaps of love and four kisses XXXX
from your always devoted
Winston."

Clementine to Winston in reply:

Blenheim Palace

"My darling ...
Je t'aime passionnement ... I feel less shy in French.
Clementine."

Clementine to Winston:

Alderley
12th September, 1909

"... The year I have lived with you has been far the happiest in my life and even if it had not been it would have been well worth living."

After a little tiff:

Winston to Clementine:

No date

"... Dearest it worries me vy much that you should seem to nurse such wild suspicions wh are so dishonouring to all the love and loyalty I bear you and will please God bear you while I breathe. They are unworthy of you and me ...

You ought to trust me for I do not love and will never love any woman in the world but you and my chief desire is to link myself to you week by week by bonds which shall ever become more intimate and profound.

Beloved I kiss your memory - your sweetness and beauty have cast a glory upon my life.

You will find me always
Your loving and devoted husband
W."

Clementine to Winston after the birth of their son Randolph on 28 May 1911, whom they called 'the Chumbolly':

33, Eccleston Square, S.W.
Whit Sunday Evening
4th June, 1911

"My Sweet Beloved Winston,
The Chumbolly and I are both very well. It is a lovely calm evening after a most sultry, airless day and I have been thinking of you with pleasure among the green trees and cool waters.

I am so happy with you my Dear. You have so transformed my life that I can hardly remember what it felt like three years ago before I knew you. Goodbye Dearest One.

Your own loving
Clemmie.''

Winston to Clementine:

France
September, 1919

''My darling one

Only these few lines to mark the eleventh time we have seen the 12th Sept. together. How I rejoice to think of my gt good fortune on that day! There came to me the greatest happiness and the greatest honour of my life . . .

My dear it is a rock of comfort to have yr love and companionship at my side. Every year we have formed more bonds of deep affection . . .

I can never express my gratitude to you for all you have done for me and for all you have been to me.

Yr ever loving and devoted
W.''

Katherine Mansfield

Katherine Mansfield (1888-1923) was a brilliant, perfect short-story writer, and her influence extended far beyond the Circle - very D. H. Lawrence - in which she moved.

She fell in love with Edward Garnet, whose twin brother Arnold she had previously planned to marry. In her Journal she expressed her feelings for him, calling him 'Husband'.

Katherine Mansfield to Edward Garnet:

September, 1908

"You are my life, now. I feel as though your kisses had absorbed my very soul into yours."

September, 1908

"When I think for one moment of what the future holds for us together, what days, and oh, my husband, what nights - I feel really that I do not belong to this earth - it's too small to hold so much."

c. October, 1908

"I shall go to bed - come soon, I feel lonely tonight, and yet almost savagely passionate. Let us go up the stairs together ... lying in your arms, I fancy the world is beating to the beating of our hearts. I love you - I love you passionately with my whole soul and body."

17th September, 1908

"You see, my beloved, you have taught me so much of the joy of life -- that the world is a glorious thing - and to be alive in it a tremendous delight - that I feel I must communicate it wherever I go."

17th October, 1908

"I feel as tho' Nature said to me - 'Now that you have found your true self - now that you are at peace with the world, accepting instead of doubting - now that you love, you can see.' "

3rd October, 1908

"Do you know, Garnet, I feel so immensely that you are the complement of me - That ours will be the Perfect Union."

After many lovers both male and female, she lived with the brilliantly clever, handsome John Middleton Murray, but he was not a satisfying lover. He abandoned her, came back and abandoned her again. He wrote in 1918:

John Middleton Murray:

"The ecstasy of love, which she required, was not health, but only a hectic hastening to death. Yet if I stood my ground against her fatal desire, she tore me to pieces by her suffering and her despair."

Lady Diana Cooper

Lady Diana Cooper, born in 1892, is the most beautiful woman of the century. She is still breathtaking.

Daughter of the 8th Duke of Rutland, she was expected to make a brilliant marriage, if not a Royal one. But she fell in love with Duff Cooper, an unknown young man with political ambitions who was in the Foreign Office.

He wrote her a poem and a letter saying:

Duff Cooper to Diana Manners:

Hanover
19th April, 1915

"By the way, I always meant to ask you whether you would marry me or not? Probably not. I am mouse-poor and should be a vile husband."

Duff Cooper to Diana Manners:

BEF
July 4th

"Three letters came from you this morning, so you do love me after all. Lovely letters from Breccles which made me laugh and one from Alan ...

I cried at his description of your sweetness, your beauty and your love for me. He expresses fear of my not fully realising the last.

Perhaps I don't. One can sometimes hardly realise the greatest fabulous wealth, and feel about your love as about a miraculous fortune which has come to me which makes me proud and happy all day long, and over which I ponder and gloat more avariciously than ever the maddest miser over his heap of gold. And it is true that I never knew how great it was until I came abroad ..."

Alan* goes on very charmingly to urge on marriage...

'... She is not only the most beautiful woman in the world, but also the best, most generous, the most warm-hearted, the most gentle, the most loyal ...'

"Damn him, he appears to think that I am hanging back. He can't think that really, but is only carried away by his own verbosity.

You surely, darling, have never doubted how madly proud and wildly happy I should always have been and always shall be to marry you under any conceivable conditions, how little I should mind poverty, how gladly I should renounce all my extravagances and vices, break my champagne glasses, throw away my cigars, tear up my cards, sell all my books - the first editions first - study the habits of buses and the intricacies of tubes to obtain that inconceivable honour ...

O, my best, you can surely see how different it would all be then. Believe, believe me how gladly I would scorn the delights and live laborious days, and indeed what would it matter then how the days were spent?"

They were married in 1919.

*There is no explanation as to who 'Alan' is.

Duff Cooper to Diana:

Brescia
In the train
26th August, 1931

"I was never so miserable at leaving you as tonight, not even that first time when I left you in New York ...

We have been so very much together these last ten days, and so wonderfully happy. In all our twelve years of marriage, I do not think there has been anything to equal it.

You grow always not only dearer to me but more necessary, and you become all the time better, wiser and more to be adored."

The Duchess of Windsor

Wallis Warfield, born in Virginia in 1896, became the woman of the century, for whom a King gave up his crown and a quarter of the world's surface because he loved her. She had been married twice before but became the wife of His Royal Highness the Duke of Windsor in France in 1937.

Her ex-husband, Ernest Simpson, wrote to her a few days after the King's Abdication.

Ernest Simpson to Mrs Simpson:

> "I did not have the heart to write before. I have felt somewhat stunned and slightly sick over recent events. I am not, however, going into that, but I want to believe - I do believe - that you did everything in your power to prevent the final catastrophe.
>
> My thoughts have been with you throughout your ordeal, and you may rest assured that no one has felt more deeply for you than I have.
>
> For a few pence each day I can keep *au courant* with your doings ..."

Later there was another:

> "... And would your life have ever been the same if you had broken it off? I mean could you possibly have settled down in the old life and forgotten the fairyland through which you had passed? My child, I do not think so."

The Duchess of Windsor:

> "Any woman who has been loved as I have been loved, and who, too, has loved, has experienced life in its fullness."

Thelma, Lady Furness

Beautiful, with an almost identical twin, Thelma and Gloria Morgan, born in 1897, looked like two magnolias.

When Thelma was Viscountess Furness she met the charming, fascinating, Prince of Wales. Soon they were dancing together every night and falling in love.

Thelma joins a party the Prince is taking on Safari in Africa. She writes of their Camp for about forty of them and says:

> "After dinner was over our party soon broke up, each going to his own tent or gathering in small groups for a final pipe or night-cap. Early retiring and rising are the custom on safari.
>
> But not for the Prince and me. This was our enchanted time to be together. As we sat by our own fire, now little more than glowing embers, the tropic African night would come closer and closer. It is hard to convey the quality of those nights. The stars seemed close enough to touch ...
>
> The air was like a caress, silken soft. No one could remain insensitive to the vastness of the starry sky, the teeming, fecund sense of nature at its most prodiagal. As the Prince and I would feel enveloped in all this, we would instinctively draw closer as if we were the only two people on Earth; our companions became as unreal, as remote from us, as the insubstantial shadows along the jungle's edge.
>
> This was our Eden, and we were alone in it. His arms about me were the only reality; his words of love my only bridge to life. Borne

along on the mounting tide of his ardour, I felt myself being inexorably swept from the accustomed moorings of caution.

Each night I felt more completely possessed by our love, carried ever more swiftly in to uncharted seas of feeling, content to let the Prince chart the course, heedless of where the voyage would end.''

Eva Perón

Eva Perón (1919-1952), an actress, mistress, the wife of Colonel Juan Perón, the President of Argentina. She wielded a power undreamt of by any President's wife and inspired the women of the country to be madly, passionately, nationally in love with her.

When Eva died of cancer she was canonized by the people. There was an altar in every Peronist house and no saint received so much devotion.

Juan wrote to his mistress, Eva Duarte:

Prison Island
October, 1945

"My adored treasure,

Only when we are separated from those we love can we know how much we love them. Since the day I left you there with greatest pain you cannot imagine, I have not been able to calm my unhappy heart.

Now I know how much I love you and that I cannot live without you . . .

My sweetheart, I have those little pictures of you in my room and I look at them every day with tears in my eyes. Nothing must happen to you or my life will end. Take good care of yourself and don't worry about me, but love me very much because I need your love more than ever . . .

My last words in this letter will be to tell you to keep calm. Many, but many kisses to my dearest *chinita*.

Perón."

Eva Peron to her husband Juan:

On the way to Europe
In a DC4
June 6th, 1947

"I am very sad to be leaving because I am unable to live away from you, I love you so much that what I feel for you is a kind of idolatry, perhaps I don't know how to show what I feel for you, but I assure you that I fought very hard in my life with the ambition to be someone and I suffered a great deal.

But then you came and made me so happy that I thought it was a dream and since I had nothing else to offer you but my heart and my soul I gave them to you wholly but in all these three years of happiness, greater each day, I never ceased to adore you for a single hour or thank Heaven for the goodness of God in giving me this reward of your love, and I tried at all times to deserve it by making you happy.

I don't know if I achieved that, but I can assure you that nobody has ever loved or respected you more than I have.

I am so faithful to you that if God wished me not to have you in this happiness and took me away I would still be faithful to you in my death and adore you from the skies . . .

Many kisses, but many kisses . . .

Evita."

The Most Perfect Love-Letter

I wanted to finish this book with a love-letter I had written myself, but obviously I do not possess them.

So instead I will end with the most perfect love-letter ever written. As it was translated by Elizabeth Barrett Browning from the Portuguese, we do not know its author or to whom it was written.

So I dedicate it and this book to someone I loved with all my heart and will continue to love through all eternity.

"How do I love thee? Let me count the ways.
I love thee to the depth and breadth and height
My soul can reach, when feeling out of sight
For the ends of Being and ideal Grace.
I love thee to the level of every day's
Most quiet need, by sun and candle light.
I love thee freely, as men strive for Right;
I love thee purely, as they turn from Praise.
I love thee with the passion put to use
In my old griefs, and with my childhood's faith.
I love thee with a love I seemed to lose
With my lost saints - I love thee with the breath
Smiles, tears, of all my life! - and, if God choose,
I shall but love thee better after death."

COOKERY

Barbara Cartland's Health Food Cookery Book
Food for Love
Magic of Honey Cookbook
Recipes for Lovers

EDITOR OF

The Common Problems by Ronald Cartland (with a preface by
the Rt. Hon. The Earl of Selborne, P.C.)
Barbara Cartland's Library of Love
Barbara Cartland's Library of Ancient Wisdom

DRAMA

Blood Money
French Dressing

PHILOSOPHY

Touch the Stars

RADIO OPERETTA

The Rose and the Violet (music by Mark Lubbock) performed in 1942

RADIO PLAYS

*The Caged Bird: An episode in the Life of Elizabeth Empress of
Austria,* performed in 1957

GENERAL

Barbara Cartland's Book of Useless Information, with a Foreword by
The Earl Mountbatten of Burma
(in aid of the United World Colleges)
Love and Lovers (picture book)
The Light of Love (prayer book)
Barbara Cartland's Scrapbook, in aid of the Royal Photographic
Museum

VERSE

Lines on Life and Love

MUSIC

An Album of Love Songs, sung with the Royal Philharmonic
Orchestra

MAGAZINE

Barbara Cartland's World of Romance (published in the USA)

SPECIAL PUBLICATION

Love at the Helm, inspired and helped by Admiral of the Fleet Earl
Mountbatten of Burma, in aid of the Mountbatten Memorial Trust